GENERALS

Hal Rogers

FOOTBALL
HEROES

The Rourke Corporation, Inc.
Vero Beach, Florida 32964

The Rourke Corporation, Inc.
P.O. Box 3328, Vero Beach, FL 32964

Rogers, Hal 1966—
      Generals / by Hal Rogers.
           p.   cm. — (Football heroes)
      Includes bibliographical references and index.
      Summary: Discusses the increasing importance of quarterbacks in professional football and describes the accomplishments of some of the game's best, including Sid Luckman, Terry Bradshaw, and Joe Montana.
      ISBN 0-86593-154-2
      1. Quarterback (Football)—Juvenile literature. 2. Football players—United States—Biography—Juvenile literature.
[1. Quarterback (Football) 2. Football—History.] I. Title. II. Series.
GV951.3.R64 1992
796.332'25—dc20
                                                                            92-9478
                                                                            CIP
                                                                            AC

Series Editor: Gregory Lee
Editor: Marguerite Aronowitz
Book design and production: The Creative Spark, San Clemente, CA
Cover photograph: Otto Greule, Jr./ALLSPORT

Contents

Fans know that when Joe Montana licks his fingers, he's getting down to serious business—and the other team is in trouble.

The General Leads

Imagine this: You're the quarterback of a team that's just one game away from the championship. There are only three minutes left in the fourth quarter, and your opponent—ahead by a field goal—has possession of the ball. From the sidelines, you watch as the other quarterback leads a powerful drive. It looks like all might be lost—your season may be over.

But then the drive starts to slow down. It's third and 10. The other team decides to punt. The ball goes out of bounds at your five-yard line. You've got a long way to go in just a few minutes, but there's still time to make your move. And if you can stay calm under pressure, your team may still be able to win. Concentrating hard and yelling out signals to your teammates, you begin the 95-yard drive. You throw a short pass. Then you hand off the ball to your trusty running back. Another complete pass. Then another. You scramble and gain a few more yards for a first down before the tackle. You're at their 40-yard line. There is less than one minute on the clock. So far, the drive has been perfect. The plays you've practiced hour after hour are working. The coach signals to you from the sidelines. After a quick huddle, you line up. The ball is snapped. You drop back, look out into the field, and there he is: your favorite wide receiver, right where he's supposed to be. Somehow, the defense has left him wide open—the play has worked. You hit him with a perfect pass and he runs 15 yards for a touchdown. You and your team win the game!

Like a military general, the quarterback carries out the offensive attack. He tries to read the defense to anticipate their next move. With the help of the coaches, he plans and directs the strategy that will either win or lose the game. He must be a leader, able to inspire and instruct his teammates on to victory. If a quarterback wins a big game, much like a general who wins a major battle, he will become a hero.

Perhaps the quarterback gets too much credit when his team wins a game, but the opposite is also true. He shoulders much of the blame when they lose. In no other team sport does one player have so much responsibility. Even the best hitter in baseball only gets to bat about four times in a game. And a pitcher cannot play every game of the season. On a good day, the highest scorer on a basketball court makes about one fourth of the team's points. But a quarterback takes part in every offensive play of every game, except for kicking situations.

What talents must a quarterback possess to become a star? Without a strong passing arm, no quarterback will ever be able to lead his team to victory. This is the skill that got him the job in the first place. But other things add up to separate the average

Sammy Baugh was not just a great quarterback, but also has the highest career punting average—45.1 yards per kick.

"general" from the superstar. For example, a quarterback needs to know not only his own plays, but the blocking assignments of his ten offensive teammates. He must be able to read the ever-changing defensive plans of his opponent and react accordingly.

He also needs to be a quick thinker, changing a play on a moment's notice if he realizes it won't work. He must be a leader and command the respect of his teammates, or they simply won't listen when he makes the calls. He needs quick feet to move when the defense makes it into the *pocket*, the area formed by the offensive linemen who are supposed to block the opposing defensive players and protect the passer. He needs good vision to find an open receiver. He must be tough enough to ignore the pain that comes when a 250-pound rusher gets past his protection and sacks him. And he must be able to remain calm at all times.

The quarterback is the most demanding and visible position in football. And of course, the fans love him. It is for these reasons that the pro quarterback receives the highest salary and the most publicity of all football players. Says Joe Gibbs, head coach of the Washington Redskins, "If you have a guy who can play successfully at quarterback, you have a chance to win about half your games...no matter what happens in a lot of other areas. Without a quarterback, you've got a chance of winning maybe one...."

Early Greats

Football is a young sport. The first major professional league was not organized until 1920, and the NFL we know today is barely 30 years old. The early days of football were a lot different than the game played today. For one thing, players wore very little protective equipment compared to what they wear now. The rules have changed, too.

In 1933, the NFL—which had long followed the rules of college football—began to develop its own rules for play. For example, it was only then that the forward pass was permitted from any place behind the *line of scrimmage*, the imaginary line where the play begins. Imagine how different football would be today had that rule never been changed! Up until this time, running was the preferred offensive attack. The pass was saved for the third down. No team ever passed from its own 25-yard line. In addition, the *T formation*, which is a basic element of today's offense, was almost unheard of until the 1940s. In "the T," the quarterback crouches behind the center, and the fullback lines up directly behind him with two halfbacks on each side. In the early days, the offense primarily used the *single-wing formation*, which was geared to the *tailback*, the back farthest from the line of scrimmage, running or passing on almost every play. The quarterback handled the ball far less then he does today.

The position of quarterback didn't really become important until 1937, when a young Texan named Sammy Baugh was signed to the Washington Redskins. Baugh had received a lot of attention at Texas Christian University, and his passing brought excitement into the college ranks. In his first year he led the Redskins to the NFL championship—the first rookie quarterback ever to do so. Otto Graham of the Cleveland Browns is the only other professional quarterback to pilot his team to victory in his first year of play. But unlike Baugh, Graham played for the All American Conference, an early rival to the NFL. He won the conference championship in 1946—the first year of the new league, so all his opponents were rookies, too.

Sammy Baugh is considered by many football fans to be the man who revolutionized the game. His skills brought throngs of fans into the stadium, selling out

Sid Luckman revolutionized the position of quarterback with his use of the T Formation.

game after game. In 16 years, he threw 2,995 passes and 186 touchdowns. He held sixteen NFL passing records. He led the Redskins to five division titles and two league championships. No other professional quarterback changed the destiny of his team in one season or became a star so quickly. That's why football remembers Sammy Baugh—the first man to dominate the field with his passing.

Baugh was not the only star quarterback in the early days of football. He had some stiff competition from Sid Luckman of the Chicago Bears. Under the legendary coaching of George Halas, Luckman shaped the future of professional football in 1940.

Halas had used the T formation since 1920, but the rest of the league stuck with more conservative ball. The T demands an excellent passer, and Halas found that and more in Luckman. When he came to play for the Bears in 1939, he was unfamiliar with the formation. Halas felt sure, however, that Luckman was the quarterback to make his system work. He insisted that his new "general" practice and study the T until he was sure he understood it.

Luckman's first year was uneventful, but 1940 was a year to remember. In the NFL championship game against Baugh and the Redskins, the Bears used the T formation to rout their opponents 73-0—the most decisive victory in NFL history. Suddenly every team in the NFL wanted to use the T formation. Within 10 years, every pro team except the Pittsburgh Steelers had switched. And even the stubborn Steelers followed in 1952. "You could almost sense that something tremendous was going to happen that day as we assembled for the trip to Washington," said Luckman. The win may have been spectacular, but more importantly, Halas, Luckman, and the Chicago Bears changed the way football would be played forever.

The first superstar quarterback may have been Otto Graham of the Cleveland Browns, who maintained a 55.8 completion percentage.

The Star Of The Gridiron

In the years that followed the achievements of Baugh and Luckman, the quarterback became increasingly important to the success of his team. Soon it was hard to recall that there was ever a time when the quarterback did not control the game.

As the NFL became more and more popular, it was constantly challenged by up-and-coming leagues that wanted to tap professional football. In 1946, the All-American Conference (AAC) opened shop. The one team that helped give the upstart conference respectability was the Cleveland Browns. With Otto Graham as quarterback, the team reached the playoff ten times in ten years and won four league championships in the AAC. Graham was surrounded by talent, and any great quarterback only gets better with the right team. Led by coach Paul Brown, Graham worked with ends Dante Lavelli and Mac Speedie to hone his passing game. Fullback Marion Motley, one of the NFL's first black players, completed a startling offense.

In 1950, the Browns, the Baltimore Colts, and the San Francisco 49ers became part of the NFL. Some thought the Browns' success would falter when they met the competition from the older, more experienced league. But Graham and his teammates proved they were more than just upstarts. They won the NFL championship in their first year, beating the Los Angeles Rams 30-28. With Graham as quarterback, the Browns would go on to play in the next five championship games, winning two of them. The NFL does not recognize records from the AAC. But if it did, Otto Graham would rank third behind Joe Montana and Dan Marino as the highest-rated NFL quarterback. As coach Brown noted, "The test of a quarterback is where his team finishes. So Otto Graham, by that standard, was the best of all time." When Graham finally left the Browns in 1956, they had their first losing season.

In the 1950s and 1960s, football's generals were fast becoming the stars of the pro gridiron. For example, Bobby Layne of the Detroit Lions survived as a professional quarterback for 15 years. He surpassed Sammy Baugh's outstanding records for total passes attempted and completed, for total yardage, and for touchdown passes. He also piloted his team in back-to-back NFL championships against the virtually unstoppable Cleveland Browns.

Y.A. Tittle's 17-year career with the Colts, the 49ers, and the Giants earned him three NFL MVP awards and a truckload of passing records, although he never played for a team that won a championship. With his accurate passing, Bart Starr helped the Green Bay Packers become the first NFL team to win league titles in three successive years. Starr threw 294 consecutive passes without an interception during the 1964 and 1965 seasons. Starr and his teammates also won the first two Super Bowls during 1966 and 1967. But it was Johnny Unitas, a man who almost missed the chance at a career in professional football, who really turned the quarterback into a star.

General John

Fresh out of college, Unitas started a construction job and also played semipro football two nights a week for six dollars a game. He contacted a number of

Bart Starr (15) had an appropriate name—he led the powerhouse Packers to back-to-back victories in Super Bowls I and II.

professional teams looking for a chance to show his stuff, but found no immediate takers. Finally, in 1956 the Baltimore Colts decided to give him a try. As the team's second stringer, his first game appearance was a disaster. But by the end of the season, "Johnny U" was establishing himself as a quarterback to watch.

Unitas threw at least one touchdown pass in 47 consecutive games—still an NFL record. He threw for more than 300 yards in 25 games. He has thrown more touchdown passes than any other player except Fran Tarkenton, and shares the record for most seasons leading the league in touchdowns with Len Dawson.

Perhaps Unitas is best remembered for the Colts' 1958 sudden-death victory over the New York Giants for the NFL title. With just 1:56 to play, the Colts were behind 17-14. Unitas drove his team up the field within field-goal range to tie the game 17-17 with just seven seconds remaining. The game then continued into overtime, and would end when one team scored.

The Colts lost the coin toss and kicked off, but their tough defense quickly shot down the Giants. The Colts soon had the ball on their own 20-yard line. Unitas directed his team slowly up the field, until they had a second down at the Giants' 8. Then Unitas chose a daring play: a pass to tight end Jim Mutscheller near the sideline. Had he been intercepted, the game might have been lost. But the pass was completed at the 1. On the next play, Unitas handed off to running back Alan Ameche, who scored, winning the game 23-17.

When asked if he was afraid of an interception on the pass to Mutscheller, Unitas replied, "When you know what you're doing you don't get intercepted." In that and the other 210 games he played in 18 years of professional football, Unitas proved he knew exactly what he was doing.

Sid Luckman once said, "Johnny Unitas is the greatest quarterback to ever play the game. He's better than me, better than Sammy Baugh, better than anyone." As years went by, however, the competition between quarterbacks grew fiercer, and it became more difficult to choose "the greatest." Unitas was still playing when a rookie named Joe Namath came on the scene, stealing the nation's attention. And for the first time, the personality and lifestyle of a professional athlete interested the public as much as his time on the playing field.

The New Kid, A New League
In 1960, yet another league started to play professional football in the United States, the American

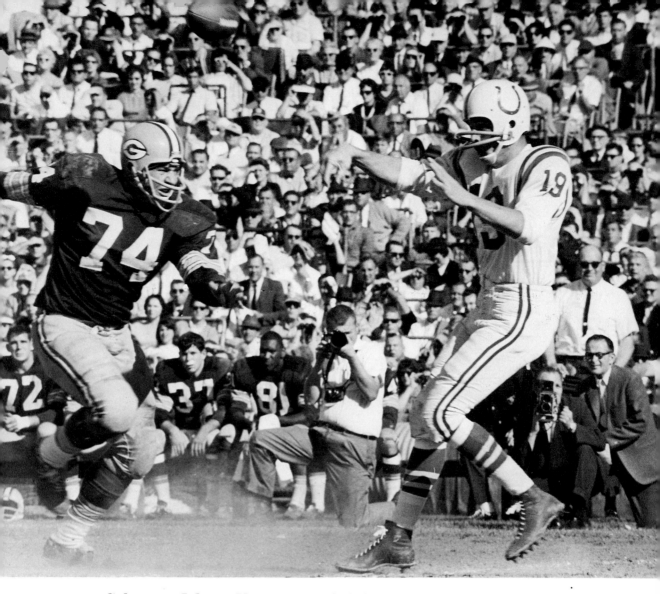

Colts star Johnny Unitas never led the NFL in passing for one season, but he is third in all-time passing yardage, with 40,239.

Football League (AFL). The AFL (today's AFC) and the NFL (now the NFC) would eventually merge to form one league, but in the 1960s there was stiff competition between the two. The New York Jets were one of the AFL's first franchises. In 1965, the Jets took on Alabama college star Joe Namath with a $427,000 contract. This was a huge amount of money at the time— particularly for a rookie who needed a knee operation.

By 1967, Namath became the first passer in pro

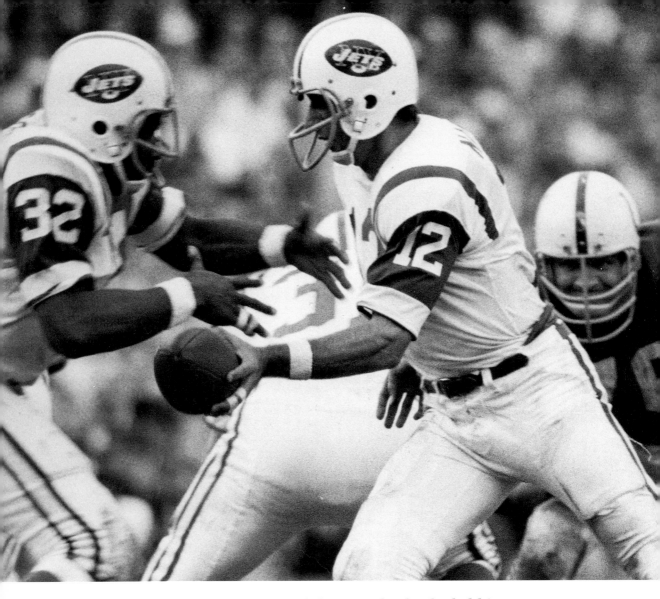

Joe Namath (12) was a colorful quarterback who led his upstart
New York Jets to the first Super Bowl victory for the AFL (now
the AFC) in 1969.

football history to throw for more than 4,000 yards. In
1968, the legendary coach Vince Lombardi (for whom
the Super Bowl trophy is named) said, "Joe Namath is
an almost perfect passer."

In 1965, the AFL and the NFL agreed to play a
championship game against each other. This game
would eventually become known as the Super Bowl.
When the AFL's New York Jets made it to Super Bowl
III in 1969, the NFL was still considered the better
league. The Jets were to meet the Baltimore Colts,

who—even with an injured Unitas—were a heavy favorite to win. But the AFL had Joe Namath, a quarterback who had the nerve to announce to the public that his team would win. "We're going to beat the Colts on Sunday," announced a confident Namath. "I *guarantee* it."

By game day, the Colts had become 19½ point favorites. Namath's teammates were angry about his gutsy promises. In the first half, Earl Morrall, the Colts' second string quarterback—threw three interceptions. Namath was cool and confident. While the Colts tried to fight back, the Jets played conservative ball. Namath's longest pass was just 39 yards. He completed 17 of 28 passes and led his team in a steady attack. The Jets scored a touchdown in both the second and third quarters, while the Colts couldn't make it onto the scoreboard. Finally, in the fourth quarter, the ailing Johnny Unitas replaced Morrall. He gave the Colts their only touchdown, but it was too late. The Jets scored a field goal and won the game 16-7.

If ever a game produced a superstar, this was it. In one game, Namath made the AFL respectable. After an uneventful season the following year, Namath was ready to enter the 1971 season with a vengeance. Unfortunately, in the opening exhibition game, he was hit in the knee by a Detroit Lions' linebacker. The injury was so severe that his career was virtually ended. For a quarterback with such a short career, Namath has a solid reputation with football experts. In his own words, Namath suggests the reason why: "I may not have a lot of victories, but I'm always a winning quarterback." He may have lost a few battles, but he won the war.

The Dallas Cowboys were a potent team in the 1970s, and Roger Staubach was their general.

Dominating The Seventies

It is very difficult to compare today's players with those of early professional football. Since the 1960s, players have become bigger, stronger, faster. Coaching techniques have improved, and today players are even sharpening their reflexes with the use of computers. But teams—as well as quarterbacks—can only be judged fairly against their current competition. To be judged "the best," a quarterback and his team must prove themselves over a long period of time.

In the 1970s, two quarterbacks and their teams stood this test of time. One team, the Dallas Cowboys, was so confident of its reputation in professional football that they called themselves "America's Team." Led by 1963 Heisman Trophy winner Roger

Quarterback Trivia

Q: *Who was the oldest quarterback to play professional football?*
A: *George Blanda's 20-year career ended in 1975 when he was 48 years old. Blanda was also a place kicker, which gave him more opportunities to score a huge number of points. With 2,002 points, Blanda ranks as the number one scorer in pro football history.*

Q: *What is the longest pass ever completed in football history?*
A: *Six quarterbacks have hurled the ball 99 yards for a touchdown. The first to do it was Frank Filchock of the Washington Redskins in 1939.*

Quarterbacks take some hard hits, like Miami's Bob Griese in Super Bowl VIII. But Griese had the last word: his Dolphins beat the Vikings for their second Super Bowl victory in a row.

Staubach and legendary coach Tom Landry, the Cowboys certainly captured the country's attention. The Dallas team had always been "next year's champions" until Staubach came to play. In his 10 years with the team, the Cowboys missed the playoffs only once.

Staubach is ranked today as the fourth greatest quarterback in NFL history. With two Super Bowl wins and four NFC championships to his credit, it isn't any wonder. Tom Landry once said a successful quarterback must be able to make the big plays when his team needs them. "This is the characteristic of all great quarterbacks—they can pull off the play that they need when they need it most." Staubach is famous for doing just that. But just as often, Staubach had such tight control of the game that a "Hail Mary" pass wasn't necessary. This was the case in both winning Super Bowls he quarterbacked. In Super Bowl VI, the Cowboys beat the Miami Dolphins 24-3; six years later, they beat the Denver Broncos 27-10.

Staubach was certainly a skilled passer, but he is best known for his intellect and leadership. Although Landry called the plays from the sidelines, Staubach was allowed to change a play if he thought something else would work better. Landry would joke, "Roger can always change the play, as long as his play works." And it usually did, in part because his teammates believed in him as both a play caller and a passer.

Great Field Battles

The closest thing yet to a Super Bowl rivalry has to be the matchup between the Dallas Cowboys and the Pittsburgh Steelers of the '70s. And with two of the best quarterbacks of all time playing for these teams, the rivalry was fierce. The two teams met in Super Bowl XIII for the second time in four seasons. Pittsburgh, with the accurate and strong arm of quarterback Terry Bradshaw, had yet to lose a championship. And this year would be no different, although Staubach's persistence came close to ending the Steeler's hold on the Vince Lombardi trophy. His team was behind 35-17, but in the last six minutes of the game the Cowboys closed the gap 35-31. That was Staubach—a quarterback who could certainly come through with the big play. Unfortunately for the Cowboys the clock ran out too soon, and the Steelers won their third Super Bowl.

*Hall of Fame quarterback Terry Bradshaw demolished opponents
in four Super Bowls with his gutsy passing.*

Bradshaw and the Steelers won four
championships in six years. Many credit this success to
the strong arm of Bradshaw, but the Steelers of the '70s
were an almost perfect team. The frightening defense,
led by Mean Joe Greene, became known as "the Steel
Curtain," and it terrified opponents throughout most of
the decade. Bradshaw had two wide receivers, Lynn
Swann and John Stallworth, who always seemed to be
exactly where he wanted them. Together with the
talents of running back Franco Harris, Bradshaw could

Lynn Swann (88) and John Stallworth (not shown) were dangerous pass receivers, the favorite targets of Terry Bradshaw.

do no wrong.

Bradshaw had been the number one draft pick in 1970 when the losing Steelers chose him for their team. From the beginning Bradshaw had a sure arm, but a good quarterback also needs experience in reading the defense, calling the plays, and knowing when to release the ball. The rookie Bradshaw used his first few seasons to sharpen his skills. By 1972, when Franco Harris joined the team, the Steelers were on their way to becoming a legend.

Bradshaw and Harris became known for their heart-stopping plays, including the famed 1972 playoff game's "immaculate reception." It was the Steelers' fourth down and they were on their own 40-yard line. They were behind 7-6 with only 20 seconds remaining. Bradshaw threw a desperation pass to halfback John Fuqua. Fuqua and Oakland Raider Jack Tatum jumped for the ball. It ricocheted off Tatum's helmet, and Harris caught it just as it fell dangerously close to the ground. He ran, untouched, for the touchdown that won the game.

The Bradshaw-Swann connection was no less spectacular. In their first Super Bowl against the Cowboys, Bradshaw completed four passes to Swann that added up to an incredible 161 yards.

The Tarkenton Touch

While Staubach and Bradshaw were winning championships, another great quarterback and his team just couldn't achieve a Super Bowl win. Fran Tarkenton was in command of the Minnesota Vikings for 13 years, and spent another five with the New York Giants. During that time he threw more touchdowns than any other quarterback in NFL history.

Tarkenton joined the Vikings in 1961. In the beginning, no one expected much from him. He was small for a quarterback, but he was a *scrambler*. An NFL quarterback often passes from the pocket. When it looks like he may be sacked by pass rushers, the quarterback tries to leave the pocket by running around or "scrambling." The Vikings had a weak offensive line when Tarkenton started, so there was never much of a pocket. Scrambling quickly became his style, and he gained the nickname, "Scramblin' Fran."

At first this technique annoyed coach Norm Van Brocklin, himself a former quarterback with an

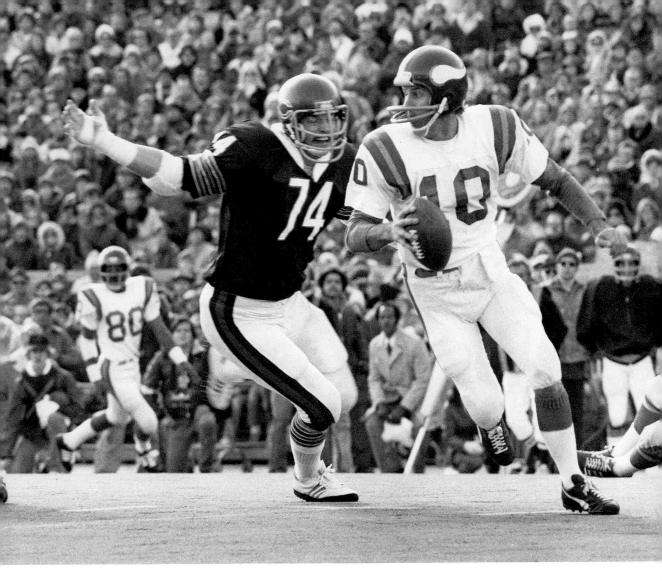

The man with the most touchdown passes—and the sweetest scramble—in NFL history is Fran Tarkenton of the Vikings.

impressive record with the L.A. Rams. Said Van Brocklin, "We'd like Francis to throw more out of the pocket, but Francis has this ability to scramble around. It's a plus." It soon became clear that this technique was working when Tarkenton's statistics started looking good. The defensive linemen would tire out as Tark scrambled around until he found an open receiver. Suddenly, out of nowhere, a new kind of quarterback was making his mark in the NFL—the *roll-out passer*, who moved toward the sideline before passing rather

Like a smart general, the Raiders' Jim Plunkett surveys the defense during Super Bowl XV. His team beat the Philadelphia Eagles 27-10, and were the first wild-card team to win the big one.

than dropping into the pocket.

Scrambling seemed to protect Tarkenton, who was only hurt once late in his career. He may not have had the strongest arm in football, but he was accurate and smart. In 18 years, Tarkenton completed 3,686 passes for 47,003 yards and 342 touchdowns—all records. And with the help of Tarkenton, the Vikings went to the Super Bowl three times. Unfortunately, Tarkenton never saw a win in the big game. He is the greatest player in Super Bowl history to never have won that most-cherished victory.

Moving into the 1980s, other stars began to emerge. Jim Plunkett, a Heisman Trophy winner, had some rough years in New England and San Francisco. In the '70s it didn't look like he'd amount to much. Then in 1978, the Oakland Raiders contacted him. Plunkett came off the bench to lead the Raiders to two Super Bowl victories in 1981 and 1984. In the first, he threw an 80-yard pass to Kenny King that still stands as the longest scoring play in Super Bowl history. In that game his team became the only wild-card team to ever win the championship. And it was largely because Plunkett had come in as a mid-season starter that the team's luck began to turn around.

Then there was Dan Fouts. Working with former 49er coach Bill Walsh, Fouts became the strongest part of the San Diego Chargers. The team never made it to the Super Bowl, although in 1980 and 1981 they played in the final round of the AFC championships. Fouts led the league for yards gained in four consecutive seasons. He is second only to Fran Tarkenton in career yards gained. The lesson seems to be that a quarterback cannot be judged simply by how many championships he has won.

*Quarterback Mark Rypien came back from injuries and coaching
doubts to win the 1992 Super Bowl.*

Today's Best

The NFL rates the performance of its quarterbacks on completion percentage, average gain, touchdown percentage, and interception percentage. If we use these standards to judge these men throughout the history of football, the four all-time NFL leaders were still active in 1991.

Leading The Troops

The '80s and '90s have been exciting years for professional football with the likes of Joe Montana, Dan Marino, John Elway, Warren Moon, and Boomer Esiason calling the plays for their teams. Never before has the competition been so stiff, and never before have quarterbacks achieved such legendary status—or received such incredible salaries.

Only in the last decade has a black quarterback played in the Super Bowl: Doug Williams of the Washington Redskins. In just one quarter, Williams threw four touchdown passes and won the MVP award. Other African-American quarterbacks have also made their marks in the NFL. Two of the NFL's best signal callers, Randall Cunningham and Warren Moon, are part of the small but growing number of blacks who command their teams on the playing field. In fact, no team relies as heavily on a single player as the Philadelphia Eagles do on quarterback Randall Cunningham. In 1990 he threw 30 touchdowns and ran for 942 yards—just 26 shy of the single-season record. In the same year, he completed 271 of 465 passes for 3,466 yards while throwing only 13 interceptions.

Randall Cunningham is a rising star for the Philadelphia Eagles. He is one of the best running quarterbacks in the NFL.

People expected great things of Cunningham in 1991, but he was injured early in the season, and he was replaced by a seasoned general, Jim McMahon. McMahon had led the 1985 Chicago Bears to victory in Super Bowl XX. The Eagles finished the '91 season with a respectable record, and the often ailing but always tough McMahon helped prove that the Eagles are a team that can pull itself together, even without Cunningham.

Warren Moon of the Houston Oilers started making a name for himself late in his career. Once out of college, Moon played six years with the Canadian Football League's Edmonton Eskimos. It was when he made the move to the NFL, however, that he started

Houston's Warren Moon led the NFL in passing in 1990, with 4,689 yards and a 62.0 completion percentage.

getting noticed. With the Oilers, Moon perfected the *run-and-shoot offense*. Using this scheme, the offense sends out four wide receivers, greatly increasing the amount of coverage the defense must put together to stop a completed pass. Moon is the perfect quarterback for such an offense, because he is an excellent passer and scrambler. Together with a swift and evasive set of receivers, the Oilers have become a team to be reckoned with. Since the Oilers started using the run-and-shoot, Moon's statistics have sailed ahead of other quarterbacks. In 1990, at the age of 34, he led the league for attempts, completions, and yards gained. He held the season record for most yards gained in a single game with 527 against Kansas City. He threw more touchdowns—33—than any other passer in the league. Randall Cunningham, the runner-up, threw 30.

The Denver General

Moon and the Oilers were serious Super Bowl contenders in 1991, until they met John Elway and the Denver Broncos. Elway has made a name for himself with impressive drives in the final minutes of AFC playoff games. In 1986, he took the Broncos 98 yards in 15 plays to score a last-second touchdown that tied the score against the Cleveland Browns. This great moment in football history has since been called "the drive." Denver won in overtime, and Elway's team went on to the Super Bowl. The following year was a repeat performance against the very same team, and the Broncos were back in the Super Bowl.

Unfortunately, like the Vikings of the 1970s, this is one team that can't seem to win "the big one." But in 1992, Bronco fans witnessed yet another Elway playoff drive. With 2:07 to play, Houston punted for the first time and the ball went out of bounds at Denver's two-yard line. The Broncos were down by one point with 98 yards to go and no timeouts. Things looked good for Houston, except that Elway was on the other team.

On fourth down with six yards to go at Denver's 28, Elway broke out of the pocket and scrambled seven yards for a first down. With 59 seconds left, it was another fourth down with a 10-yard gain to Denver's 35. The Oiler defense thought Elway would run again, but this time he sent a pass to wide receiver Vance Johnson, whose defender had left him open. Johnson gained 44 yards to the Houston 21. Denver sent kicker David Treadwell out for a field goal, and the Broncos won 26-24.

Counting the 1991 playoff victory, Elway had led his team to 19 fourth-quarter comeback victories. Says Bronco head coach Dan Reeves, "When you've got

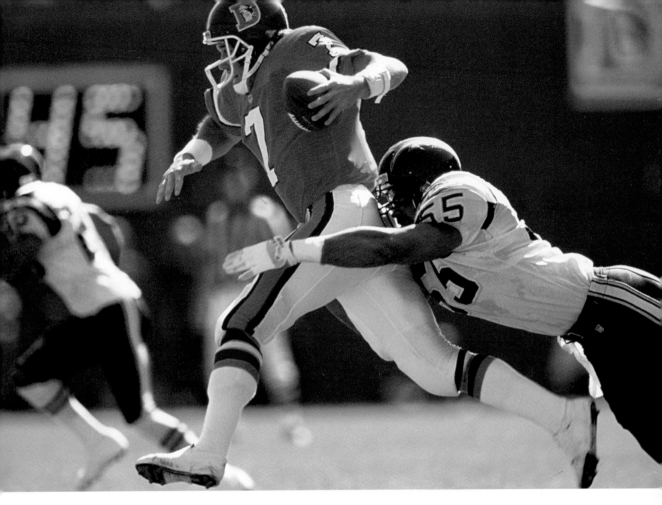

John Elway is a respected quarterback, but he has been frustrated by three Super Bowl defeats.

number 7, anything is possible....I don't think...I've seen a team go 97 yards with no timeouts to win a game." It was too bad Warren Moon had to witness it. The Oiler quarterback performed well in defeat, completing 27 of 36 passes for 325 yards and three touchdowns.

Jim Kelly of the Buffalo Bills, like Elway, started his career with the NFL in 1983. And they weren't the only two superstars to come from that year. Dan Marino, Tony Eason, Todd Blackledge, and Ken O'Brien were members of the same class. Never before had so many spectacular college quarterbacks been eligible for the draft at the same time. Jim Kelly was chosen in the first round, after Elway and Todd Blackledge. After playing two years with the short-lived USFL football league,

Although Jim Kelly lost back-to-back Super Bowls in 1991 and 1992, many fans still expect great things from him in the future.

Kelly came to the Bills. As quarterback for the Bills, Kelly helped turn the team around. After many losing seasons, the team began to win. In 1988 they won 11 of 12 games with Kelly giving the orders. But it wasn't until 1990 that Kelly really started to show the world what a football four-star general looks like. And some experts think he's still getting better.

Kelly took the Bills to back-to-back Super Bowls in 1990 and 1991. Although they did not bring home the trophy either year, Super Bowl XXV was one of the toughest and most exciting NFL championships ever. While Moon is known for the run-and-shoot, the Bills use the *no-huddle offense*. When the offense doesn't huddle, the defense doesn't have time to anticipate their opponents' next play or send in new players. They have to act fast. Kelly calls the plays at the line of scrimmage. In fact, he is the first player since Jim Plunkett who calls *all* of his own plays. And with the winning seasons of '90 and '91 to consider, Coach Marv Levy isn't complaining.

In 1991, another quarterback from the class of '83—Dan Marino—signed a five-year, $25-million contract extension with the Miami Dolphins. This made him the highest-paid player in football history. From his first season, Marino was a star. The Miami Dolphins are a solid team with a great coach, Don Shula. Marino started halfway through his rookie season, teaming up with a group of fine receivers including Mark Duper, Mark Clayton, Nat Moore, and Tony Nathan. Together, they formed a superior offense. In his rookie year, Marino was the AFC's leading passer, completing 173 of 296 passes for 2,210 yards and 20 touchdowns. But this would be nothing compared to the following year.

From the beginning of the 1984 season, Marino couldn't be stopped. As a second-year quarterback, he was already challenging records. George Blanda and

The Dolphins' Dan Marino is one of the highest-paid superstars in the NFL.

Y.A. Tittle, who both played in the 1960s, shared the record for most touchdowns thrown in a season (36). After 12 games in 1984, Marino had thrown 32 touchdowns. One week later against the Jets, he tied the NFL record. Then, with just three games left in the season, Marino and the Dolphins faced the L.A. Raiders. In 57 attempts, Marino completed 35 passes for an incredible 470 yards and four touchdowns. He had thrown 40 touchdowns in one season—a new NFL record. And there were still two games left.

The next week he increased the record to 44. In the final game of the season against the Dallas Cowboys, Marino threw four touchdowns for the third week in a row. He finished with 48, becoming the first quarterback in the NFL to throw more than 5,000 yards in a single season. And with a record of 14-2, he took the Dolphins through the playoffs and into the Super Bowl—against the San Francisco 49ers and Joe Montana.

It was a classic matchup between two powerful teams—exactly what the Super Bowl is supposed to be. But even the Dolphins and Marino couldn't stop the red-hot San Francisco offense. Marino was forced to play catch-up as Montana and the near-perfect 49er offense blew by the Dolphin linemen. The 49ers won 38-16.

Today, the Dolphins are building a stronger defense and have a skilled running back named Sammie Smith to help Marino bring the team closer to the Super Bowl. Marino continues to be one of the most dangerous passers in the NFL, but the Dolphins haven't quite pulled together a championship team. History shows that it takes more than a great quarterback to win games, and Joe Montana—in his incredible career with the San Francicso 49ers—has always had a good team to back him up.

Many football fans consider Joe Montana of the San Francisco 49ers to be the greatest quarterback of all time.

Montana Magic

In the 1979 draft, 81 choices were made before the 49ers took Montana near the end of the third round. A lot of teams passed up a young man who turned out to be history's greatest quarterback. Coach Bill Walsh and the 49ers were looking for a quarterback to help rebuild a losing team. As Walsh says, he soon knew that Montana would work with the offense he wanted to build.

By 1980 the 49er offense was beginning to take shape. Montana started in seven of 10 games that year. His specialty, the short, controlled pass with Dwight Clark as receiver, became a big part of the offense. Walsh worked slowly with Montana to build the kind of quarterback he needed. Then he built the offensive team to match Montana's skills: a knack for escaping the pass rush, consistency, a talent for coming back from behind, and the ability to throw while in the grasp of the opponent.

It all fell into place. The big game was against the Dallas Cowboys for the NFC championship. In one play, three defensive players were hanging on to Montana. Undaunted, he threw an off-balance throw to Clark, who caught it and ran for a touchdown. The 49ers beat the Cowboys and were on their way to their first Super Bowl, where they beat the Cincinnati Bengals. Then, in the 1985 Super Bowl against the Dolphins, running back Roger Craig set a Super Bowl record by scoring three touchdowns: two on receptions from Montana and one on a run of two yards. Dwight Clark had six receptions for 77 yards, while Russ Francis had five for 60. Montana hit all the right receivers with his accurate arm. He completed 24 of 35 passes for a Super Bowl record of 331 yards and three touchdowns.

In 1985, the 49ers lost in the NFC wild-card game, and in 1986 Montana was out with a back injury for 55 days. But in 1987, the 49ers could seemingly do no wrong and ended the season 13-2. But they were upset by Minnesota in the NFC divisional playoff. In 1988, Montana was slowed by injuries to his elbows, ribs, back, and knees, but the team still made it to the Super Bowl. And if there was a question about whether Montana was as good as he used to be, the final drive against the Bengals—92 yards in 11 plays—answered it. With 34 seconds left, he sent a 10-yard pass to wide receiver John Taylor, who went in for the touchdown. Montana helped wide receiver Jerry Rice win MVP awards after compiling 11 catches for a Super Bowl record 215 yards.

In 1989, Montana finished with the best season any quarterback ever had. He received the highest NFL rating and the third-highest completion percentage (70.2) in history. The startling combination of Montana and Jerry Rice galloped through another Super Bowl, beating the Denver Broncos 55-10. Montana completed 22 of 29 passes for 297 yards and a new Super Bowl record of five touchdowns.

The 1990 season was another stellar year for Montana and the 49ers. They closed the regular season 14-2, and came within a field goal of making a third consecutive appearance in the Super Bowl. In 1991, however, the 49ers lost Montana early in the season to an injury.

Montana leads the pack when it comes to statistics. He's never been intercepted in a Super Bowl, he has the highest career quarterback rating of all time, and he is second only to the Cleveland Browns' Bernie Kosar in lowest lifetime interception rate. Among quarterbacks with a minimum of 1,500 passes, Montana is the only one to have thrown twice as many career touchdowns as interceptions. But perhaps the most impressive statistic is that during his time with the NFL, he was responsible for 23 fourth-quarter comeback victories. Montana never loses his cool. Teammates and coaches alike respect him for his ability to play well under pressure, especially when everything is on the line in the fourth quarter.

Who's The Best?

Is Montana the best quarterback ever? A large number of coaches and players think he is. Johnny Unitas is another contender for "the greatest ever." But football today is a lot different then it was when Unitas played. For example, changes in the rules allow for freer passing lanes. Today the receiver has greater protection from the defense, players who can no longer "bump-and-run" without being called for pass interference. That makes it easier for the quarterback to hit his target. On the other hand, more is expected from today's signal callers. Former Green Bay Packer coach Lindy Infante notes, "We're asking quarterbacks to do things nowadays that 10 years ago I don't think we as coaches ever thought guys were capable of doing. To me there's an emphasis placed on the guy's brain."

Does it really matter who is the best quarterback in history? There is such a wide variety from which to choose: Baugh, Montana, Luckman, Moon, just to name a few. The important thing is that the quarterback has held our interest for more than 50 years, and it doesn't look like that will change. The quarterback is the one who calls the signals, who commands the team. He's the one who gets the credit when his team wins, and the blame when they lose. As Boomer Esiason, quarterback for the Cincinnati Bengels, puts it, "Everyone knows the quarterback. He's the American hero. What a great thing to be....There's nothing quite like it."

Stats

All-Time Leaders: Touchdown Passes			
	Years	Touchdowns	Int
Fran Tarkenton	18	342	266
Johnny Unitas	18	290	253
Sonny Jurgensen	18	255	189
Dan Fouts	15	254	242
John Hadl	16	244	268
Joe Montana	12	242	123
Dan Marino	8	241	136
Len Dawson	19	239	183
George Blanda	26	236	277
John Brodie	17	214	224
Terry Bradshaw	14	212	210
Y.A. Tittle	15	212	221
Jim Hart	19	209	247
Roman Gabriel	15	201	149
Ken Anderson	16	197	160
Norm Snead	15	196	253
Joe Ferguson	18	196	209
Bobby Layne	15	196	243
Ken Stabler	15	194	222
Bob Griese	14	192	172
Sammy Baugh	16	187	203
Dave Krieg	11	184	136
Craig Morton	18	183	187

All-Time NFL Quarterback Leaders

	Att	Comp	Yards	TD	Int
Joe Montana	4579	2914	34,998	242	123
Dan Marino	4181	2480	31,416	241	136
Jim Kelly	2088	1251	15,730	105	72
Boomer Esiason	2687	1520	21,381	150	98
Roger Staubach	2958	1685	22,700	153	109
Neil Lomax	3153	1817	22,771	136	90
Sonny Jurgensen	4262	2433	32,224	255	189
Len Dawson	3741	2136	28,711	239	183
Dave Krieg	3291	1909	24,052	184	136
Jim Everett	2038	1154	15,345	101	73
Ken O'Brien	2878	1697	20,444	109	78
Ken Anderson	4475	2654	32,838	197	160
Danny White	2950	1761	21,959	155	132
Bart Starr	3149	1808	24,718	152	138
Fran Tarkenton	6467	3686	47,003	342	266
Bernie Kosar	2363	1364	16,450	85	62
Dan Fouts	5604	3297	43,040	254	242
Warren Moon	3025	1701	22,989	134	112
Tony Eason	1564	911	11,142	61	51
Jim McMahon	1840	1056	13,398	77	66
Randall Cunningham	2253	1230	15,399	107	71
Bert Jones	2551	1430	18,190	124	101
Johnny Unitas	5186	2830	40,239	290	253
Otto Graham	1565	872	13,499	88	94
Frank Ryan	2133	1090	16,042	149	111

Glossary

LINE OF SCRIMMAGE. The imaginary line where the play begins, running through the center of the ball, from sideline to sideline.

NO-HUDDLE OFFENSE. An offensive strategy that doesn't use the huddle, thus the defense doesn't have time to anticipate their opponents' next play or send in new players.

POCKET. The area formed by the offensive linemen who are supposed to block the opposing defensive players and protect the passer.

ROLL-OUT PASSER. A quarterback who moves toward the sideline before passing instead of dropping into the pocket.

RUN-AND-SHOOT OFFENSE. An offensive scheme where the offense sends out four wide receivers, greatly increasing the amount of coverage the defense must put together to stop a completed pass.

SCRAMBLE. The action of leaving the pocket to avoid being sacked by pass rushers. The quarterback runs around, or scrambles, to avoid being tackled.

T FORMATION: The basic element of today's offense when the quarterback crouches behind the center, and the fullback lines up directly behind him with two halfbacks on each side. In the early days, the offense primarily used the *single-wing formation*, which was geared to the tailback. The quarterback handled the ball far less than he does today.

Bibliography

Books

Anderson, Dave. *The Story of Football.* New York: William Morrow and Company, Inc., 1985.

Duroska, Lud, ed. *Great Pro Quarterbacks.* New York: Grosset & Dunlap, 1974.

Gutman, Bill. *Pro Football's Record Breakers.* New York: Pocket Books, 1987.

Hollander, Zander, ed. *The Complete Handbook of Pro Football.* New York: Signet, 1991.

Meserole, Mike, ed. *The 1992 Information Please Sports Almanac.* Boston: Houghton Mifflin.

The Official National Football League 1991 Record & Fact Book. New York: Workman Publishing Co., 1991.

Periodicals

Zimmerman, Paul. "The Big Moon Launch." *Sports Illustrated,* November 5, 1990: 68.

Zimmerman, Paul. "The Ultimate Winner" (Joe Montana). *Sports Illustrated,* August 13, 1990: 74.

Photo Credits

Index